Puppy Show

by Sallie Carson

Illustrated by Karol Kaminski

PEARSON

Scott
Foresman

Editorial Offices: Glenview, Illinois • Parsippany, New Jersey • New York, New York
Sales Offices: Needham, Massachusetts • Duluth, Georgia • Glenview, Illinois
Coppell, Texas • Sacramento, California • Mesa, Arizona

puppies

Abby and Caleb giggled as the puppies jumped around them, but Mom looked serious.

"Raising puppies is a big job," she said. "Puppies need food and water. They need walks and baths. Most of all, they need to learn to behave."

---

behave: act properly

2

puppy

Caleb picked up his wiggling puppy. "Don't worry," Caleb said. "Puppy training is our 4-H project. We can start tomorrow."

"Yes," said Abby. "When the puppies are six months old, they can enter the puppy show. My puppy will win!"

wiggling: moving and twisting back and forth
4-H: a club for boys and girls

The next day, the children put leashes on the puppies. When the puppies tried to run away, Caleb and Abby called "Come!" and pulled on their leashes.

4

Stay!

leash

As soon as the puppies learned one command, the children taught them a new one.

Some actions happened in the past, and some happen now. Action words help you understand when things happen.

Now	Past
pull	pulled
learn	learned
wag	wagged
stay	stayed
call	called

Caleb and Abby practiced with the puppies for a short time every day. The puppies were **a real handful**. The first thing they learned was the word *no*.

tail

After each training time, Caleb and Abby played with the puppies. The puppies wagged their tails. They liked learning. That was a good thing. Mom told the children, "**Before you know it, it will be time for the puppy show!**"

7

blue ribbon

On the day of the show, all the 4-H club members walked their puppies around the ring. The puppies heeled, sat, stayed, and came when they were called.

Abby was right. Her puppy *did* win. Every puppy won a prize!